Cookies for Kids

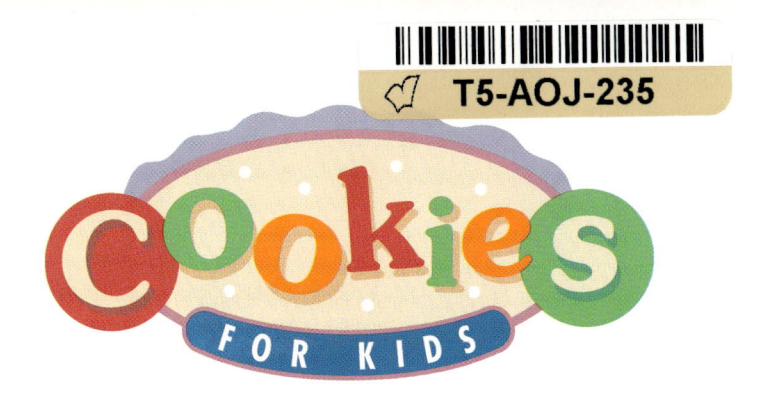

Recipe Development—Joanne Karlson
Editor—Sharon Krall
Photographer—Clive Tyler

Cookies for Kids provides ideas and easy directions for goodies kids will like and can even help make. These unique creations are suitable for holidays, birthdays, and just about any occasion you want to make special. If your child wishes to help make and decorate the cookies, review the photographs together to choose a design; they are purposely simple to minimize fuss and maximize fun. The dough and frosting recipes are basic and easy to follow with some variations. No need to invest in a host of fancy cookie cutters; these designs can be cut from a few empty food cans and a table knife. For those of you who are always short on time but still love to play, directions are provided for using purchased slice-and-bake doughs and frostings. This book is intended to smooth the way for an enjoyable cookie-making experience, with delightful results. Don't forget: embellishments and colors can be varied according to personal preferences, level of expertise, and availability of ingredients.

NOTE TO ADULTS: If a child wishes to help, we encourage you to review each recipe with your child before he or she starts. Determine the amount of adult supervision required based on his or her maturity and ability level. Adult supervision is also suggested when a child uses any household appliance.

©1994 Current, Inc., Colorado Springs, CO 80941
All rights reserved, including the right of reproduction in whole or in part.
PRINTED IN THE U.S.A
ISBN 0-944943-26-8

CONTENTS

RECIPES AND TECHNIQUES
Cookies 3
Frostings 4
Techniques 7

ANIMALS
Buddy Bear 9
Polka Pig 10
Terrific Tomcat 10
Flirty Fantail 11

NOVELTIES
Pizza Party 13
Munch-A-Saurus 14
Robo-Monsters 14
Baked Invaders 15
Clown-Around Pals 15

HOLIDAYS
Kris Krumble 19
Dandy Randy Reindeer 20
Party Packages 20
Tasty Trees 21
Cookie Canes 22
Jivin' Jack O' Lantern 22
Sassy Spider 23
Wacky Webs 25
Formal Phantom 26
Spotted Owl 26
Gobble Gobblers 27
Happy Hearts 29
Sweet Hearts 30
Chewy Ewe 30
Nest Eggs 31
Bow Tie Bunny 32

Recipes
And Techniques

BASIC SUGAR COOKIE DOUGH

A versatile dough with a delicate flavor

Makes about 2½ dozen (2" diameter)

- 2½ cups all-purpose flour
- 1 teaspoon baking powder
- ¾ teaspoon salt
- 1 cup sugar
- ½ cup margarine
- ¼ cup solid vegetable shortening
- 2 large eggs
- 1½ teaspoons vanilla extract
- 1 teaspoon butter flavoring

In a medium mixer bowl, stir together flour, baking powder, and salt. In a large mixer bowl at medium speed, beat sugar, margarine, and shortening until creamy. Add eggs, vanilla, and butter flavoring; beat well. At low speed, beat in flour mixture until well blended. Divide dough into four portions. Cover and chill for 1 hour or until firm enough to handle.

Preheat oven to 350°. On a lightly floured surface, roll one portion of dough at a time to ¼-inch thickness. Dip cutters or table knife in flour and cut cookies. Place cookies 2 inches apart on ungreased baking sheets.

Bake 9 to 11 minutes until edges are light brown. Let stand 1 minute, then remove from cookie sheets and cool completely on wire racks before decorating. NOTE: Refer to p. 7 for information about baking and cooling larger cookies.

VARIATIONS

BROWN SUGAR COOKIES—Substitute 1 cup packed brown sugar for the granulated sugar.

CHOCOLATE SUGAR COOKIES—Stir ⅓ to ½ cup unsweetened cocoa powder into the flour mixture. Cookies will not be as sweet as the basic cookie and dough may need a few extra drops of water.

BUTTERCREAM FROSTING

Excellent for use in piping and decorating

Makes about 2¾ cups

- 4 **cups powdered sugar**
- ¼ **cup butter, softened**
- ¼ **cup solid vegetable shortening**
- ¼ **cup milk**
- 1 **teaspoon vanilla extract**
- ¼ **teaspoon almond extract**
- **food color (optional)**

In a small mixer bowl at low speed, beat powdered sugar, butter, shortening, milk, vanilla, and almond extract until blended. At medium-high speed, beat until light and fluffy. If desired, beat in food color (read about adding food color, p. 6). Cover and refrigerate any leftover frosting.

CHOCOLATE BUTTERCREAM FROSTING: Sift together powdered sugar and ⅓ cup unsweetened cocoa powder. Frosting may need a few extra drops of water. Prepare as above.

NOTE: For a firmer frosting, beat in additional powdered sugar, 1 tablespoon at a time.

FLOW FROSTING

Used as a base for decorating, this dries to a firm, glazed finish.

Makes about ⅔ cup

- 2 **cups sifted powdered sugar**
- 4 **teaspoons light corn syrup**
- 4 **to 6 teaspoons milk**
- **food color (optional)**

In a small bowl, mix powdered sugar, corn syrup, and 4 teaspoons milk until blended. Add remaining milk, 1 teaspoon at a time, until consistency of chocolate syrup. If desired, stir in food color, one drop at a time. Keep bowl tightly covered until ready to use to prevent surface from forming a crust.

Using a spoon, spread frosting evenly over tops of cookies. When using candy decorations, press into place just before Flow Frosting is set or attach them with a dab of decorating frosting after Flow Frosting has completely set. Flow Frosting must be *completely dry* before adding piped frostings or gels to prevent bleeding of colors.

READY-TO-SPREAD FROSTINGS

Some ready-to-spread frostings may be quite soft at room temperature. You may wish to refrigerate decorated cookies until just before serving to support the candy decorations. Keep this in mind when planning to transport decorated cookies. Adding powdered sugar will help stiffen most frostings. You may want to test a finished cookie to avoid disappointment if refrigeration is not available. Tube frostings can be purchased with a selection of decorating tips, or use your own cake decorating bags and tips. Directions for their use follow.
While shopping for cookie ingredients, remember to purchase all the extra ingredients needed for decorating and experimenting with your chosen designs.

USING A PIPING SET

STEP 1: Cut ¼ to ½ inch off the end of a disposable bag (A). Drop in a piping tip. One-half inch of the tip should stick out.

STEP 2: Fold down the top of the bag 2 to 3 inches to form a cuff over your hand. Using a spatula, scoop frosting into the bag, filling with no more than ½ cup of frosting (B).

STEP 3: Unfold the cuff and tightly twist top of bag to force some of the frosting out into a bowl (C). This will remove air bubbles and firmly pack frosting down into the tip.

STEP 4: Hold the bag in your right hand and grasp the twist between the thumb and forefinger. Squeeze with your right hand, forcing the frosting out of the bag in an even flow (D). The left hand is used only to guide or steady the bag and tip. A left-handed person will reverse hands. The squeezing and relaxing of pressure can provide great variety to the design. If desired, practice designs on a sheet of wax paper first.

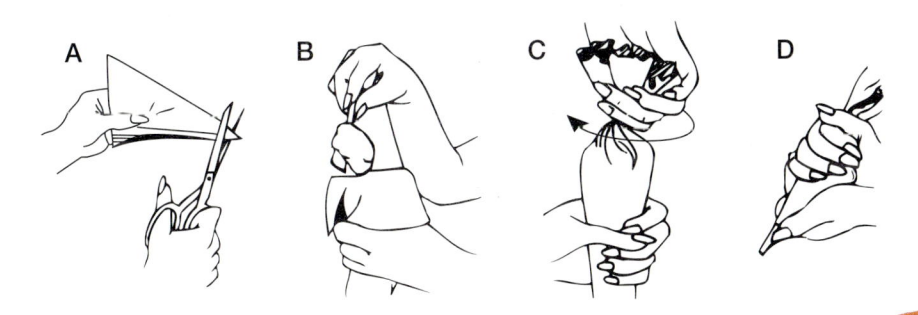

A   B   C   D

DECORATING WITH PIPING TIPS

Correct position of the bag is important to obtain satisfactory results.

DOTS: Using a round tip, hold the bag at a 90° angle with the tip slightly above the surface. Squeeze the bag, keeping the tip in the frosting until the dot is the desired size. Stop squeezing and pull away. Remove point with a wooden pick.

LINES: Using a round or star tip, glide the tip at a 45° angle, allowing it to just gently touch the surface. Make sure all loops and openings are definite so lines or designs are distinct. Stop squeezing and touch the tip to the surface to end a line.

STARS AND STAR BORDERS: Using a star tip, hold the bag at a 90° angle with the tip almost touching the surface. Squeeze to form a star, lifting slightly. Stop squeezing and pull away. Increase or decrease pressure for different star sizes. Pipe stars side by side to form a border.

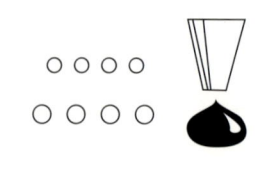

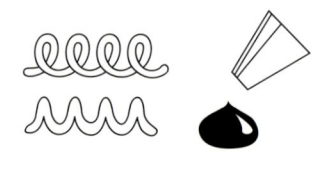

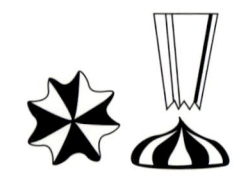

USING FOOD COLORS

Paste food color can be purchased in cake decorating supply stores, craft stores, or specialty sections of department stores. Paste food color will make deep, vivid hues, while liquid food color makes softer colors and thins the frosting. Using a wooden pick, add paste color in very tiny amounts. Add liquid food color one drop at a time to control the amount used.

TECHNIQUES

Storing Cookies: Unfrosted cookies should be stored in an airtight container in a cool place. Store decorated cookies in a single layer, loosely covered in a cool place.

Shaping Cookies: Use floured fingers to shape cookies. Cookies will be stronger and hold together better if pieces are overlapped slightly and your fingers are moistened when pinching or pressing pieces of dough together to attach legs, ears, etc.

Baking Times for Larger Cookies: Bake the suggested time, adding a minute or two to baking time if the cookies seem too soft. Because oven temperatures vary, as well as the sizes of hand-crafted cookies, closely observe cookies during the additional minutes of baking to avoid overbaking.

Cooling Larger Cookies: To minimize breakage after baking, allow cookies to remain on baking sheets 1 to 2 minutes to cool slightly, then slide a metal spatula under each cookie and release from baking sheet. Allow cookies to cool completely on the baking sheet before applying frosting.

Making Round Cookie Cutters: Bottle caps and the tops and bottoms of empty cans make excellent round cutters, especially if edges are straight and sharp.

7½ oz.	lemon juice bottle cap	=	⅞ in. diameter
1 gal.	jug cap	=	1½ in. diameter
6 oz.	tomato paste can	=	2 in. diameter
10½ oz.	condensed soup can	=	2½ in. diameter
16 oz.	vegetable can	=	3 in. diameter
3 lb.	solid vegetable shortening can	=	5 in. diameter

Making Other Shapes: To make oval shapes, find shallow, round cans you can squeeze into ovals. Some metal spice cans can be used for rectangles. Pry off the plastic top and puncture the metal bottom to allow air to escape as you are cutting out the cookies. Larger rectangles can be made by using the top of a gourmet international coffee can. Unusual shapes, such as triangles or free-form curves, can be made with a floured table knife.

Making Cookie Ornaments: To prepare cookies for hanging, cut dough into desired shapes. Dip the end of a plastic drinking straw into flour, then cut a hole near the top of the unbaked cookie. If necessary, when cookies are half-baked, remove baking sheets from the oven and quickly enlarge the holes. Return cookies to oven and complete baking. Cool and decorate. Thread a colorful piece of ribbon or yarn through each hole.

Animals

These are not any run-of-the-mill animal cookies; this creative collection of critters will make little eyes light up and smiles break out. Imaginations run wild in the making and munching of these funny, fantasy friends.

BUDDY BEAR

(pictured on p. 8)

Chocolate Sugar Cookie Dough (p. 3)
chocolate chips or raisins
chocolate-covered candies
chocolate decorating frosting in a tube
pink and blue Buttercream Frosting (p. 4) or gel in tubes
gumdrops or small round candies

Roll dough to ¼-inch thickness. Each cookie requires one 3-inch circle for the head, two ⅞-inch circles for the ears, and two small triangles for the bow tie. (See p. 7 for cutter ideas.) Place a circle on the baking sheet, attach ears by overlapping circles slightly. Add bow tie pieces. Press pieces together with lightly moistened fingers. Be sure bears are at least 2 inches apart. Press chocolate chips into dough for eyes. Bake and cool as directed.

To decorate, leave cookies unfrosted. Attach chocolate candy nose with a dab of frosting. Attach a small chocolate candy to each ear with a dab of pink frosting. Use chocolate decorating frosting and a round tip to outline the head, nose, and mouth. Frost bow tie with blue frosting, outline it with piping gel, then attach a gumdrop slice. Refrigerate to set frostings.

POLKA PIG

(pictured on p. 8)

Basic Sugar Cookie Dough (p. 3)
pink ready-to-spread frosting (p. 5)
pink decorating sprinkles
red licorice laces

small candies (Life Savers®, Skittles®)
chocolate piping gel in a tube

Roll dough to ¼-inch thickness. Each cookie requires two 1½-inch circles, one triangle for ear and three small rectangles for legs. (See p. 7 for cutter ideas.) Overlap two circles on baking sheet, then add feet and ear. Press pieces together with lightly moistened fingers. Be sure pigs are at least 2 inches apart. Follow baking and cooling instructions for large cookies (p.7).

To decorate, spread pink frosting over tops of cookies. Press pink sprinkles into frosting to produce "polka dots." Twist a 2-inch length of licorice for the tail; attach it, the candy nose, and eyes with a dab of frosting. Outline pig's body, head, and facial details with chocolate piping gel. Refrigerate to set frostings.

TERRIFIC TOMCAT

(pictured on p. 8)

Brown Sugar Cookie Dough (p. 3)
small candies (candy corn, M & M's®, red-hot candies)

pink piping gel in a tube
chocolate piping gel in a tube
yellow decorating frosting in a tube

Roll dough to ¼-inch thickness. Each cookie requires one 2½-inch circle for the head, two small triangles for ears, and one rectangle for the collar. (See p. 7 for cutter ideas.) Place circle on baking sheet; attach ears and collar. Press pieces together with lightly moistened fingers. Be sure cats are at least 2 inches apart. Bake and cool as directed.

To decorate, leave unfrosted. Attach eyes, nose, and mouth with small dabs of frosting. Use pink gel to add depth to ears. Use chocolate piping gel to outline head, ears, whiskers, and center of eyes. Spread yellow decorating frosting on collar and press heart-shaped red-hot candies or other candy "jewels" into frosting. Refrigerate to set frostings.

FLIRTY FANTAIL

(pictured on p. 8)

Basic Sugar Cookie Dough (p. 3)
Flow Frosting (p. 4)
food color (p. 6)
multicolored decorating sprinkles

piping gel in a tube
small round candies (M & M's®, Necco® candies, Runts®)

Roll dough to ¼-inch thickness. Each cookie requires one whole and one-half 3-inch circle and two triangles. (See p. 7 for cutter ideas.) Place one circle on the baking sheet, attach half circle fin to one side, then add top and bottom triangle fins. Press pieces together with lightly moistened fingers. Be sure fish are at least 2 inches apart. Bake and cool as directed.

To decorate, spread Flow Frosting evenly over tops of cookies. Before frosting sets, add sprinkles and candies to resemble "scales" and small candies for eyes and mouth. After frosting sets, pipe gel around the outer edges of fins, adding details to each. Refrigerate to set frostings.

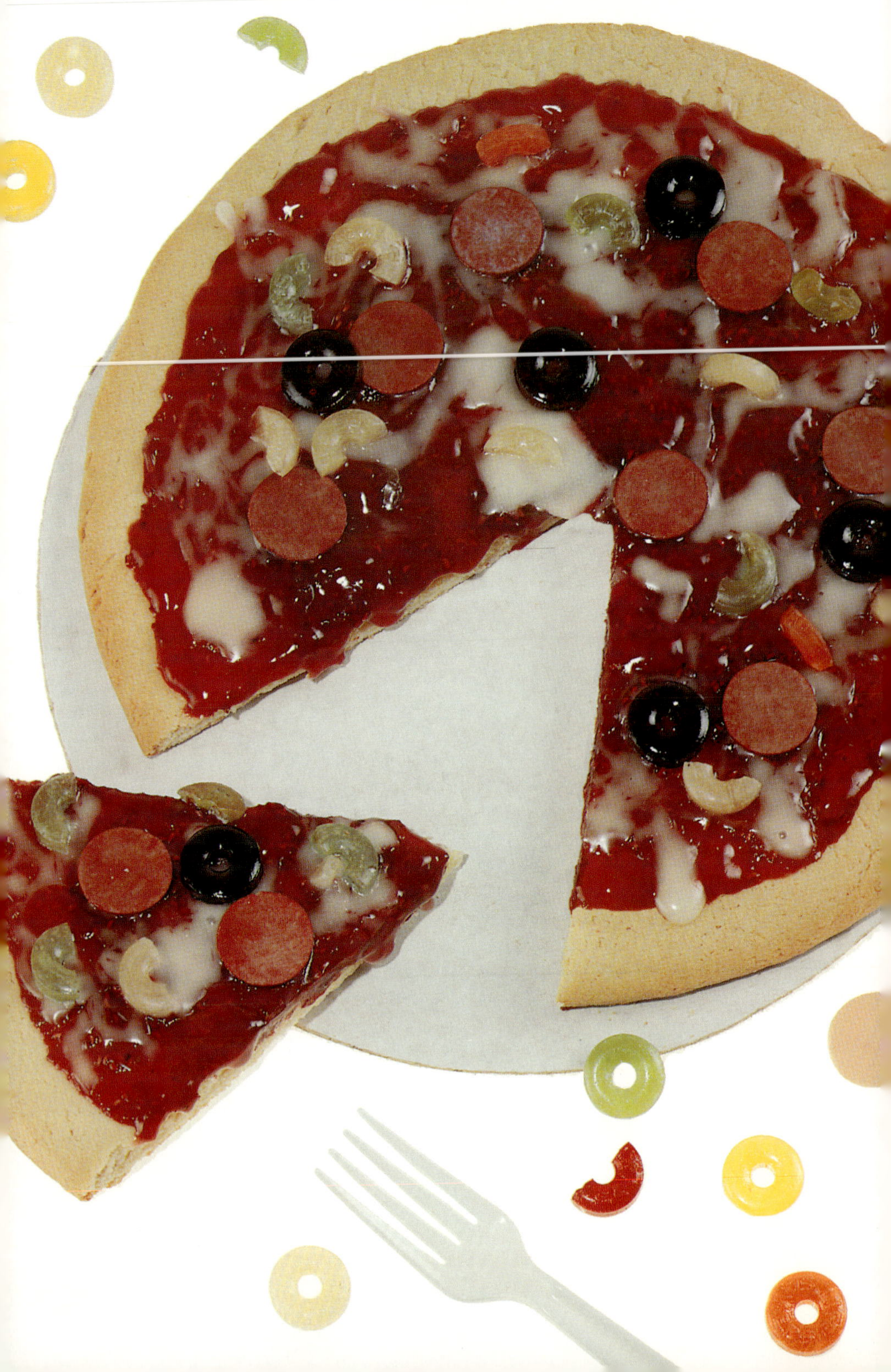

Novelties

PIZZA PARTY

(pictured on p. 12)

20 oz. (1 lb. 4 oz.) roll of refrigerated chocolate chip cookie dough
12" diameter foil pizza pan
strawberry or raspberry jam
Life Savers® candies (some broken in half)
Necco® candies
"Mock Mozzarella" Drizzle (recipe follows)

Preheat oven according to package directions. Slice cookie dough ¼-inch thick and arrange slices in a single layer on foil pizza pan, fitting pieces together and pressing evenly with floured fingers to within 1 inch of outer edge of pan. (This allows for spreading of the dough while baking.) Bake 20 to 25 minutes until lightly browned and set 2 inches from the edge of pan. Carefully slide a baking sheet under the foil pan and remove from oven. Cool cookie in pan on a wire rack.

To decorate, spread jam over top of cookie. Sprinkle on candies to look like vegetables and meat; spoon "Mock Mozzarella" Drizzle over the top. Refrigerate until firm, about 30 minutes. Cut into wedges to serve.

"MOCK MOZZARELLA" DRIZZLE

Melt *2 ounces cut-up white chocolate or white candy coating* and *½ to 1 teaspoon solid vegetable shortening* in the top of a double boiler or in a bowl that fits snugly over a saucepan. The water in the bottom pan should be at least 1" deep and hot, but not boiling. Stir the mixture frequently with a wooden or plastic spoon until melted. If mixture is too thick to drizzle, add *an additional ¼ teaspoon solid vegetable shortening*.

MUNCH-A-SAURUS

(pictured on p. 16 and 17)

Basic Sugar Cookie Dough (p. 3)
Buttercream Frosting (p. 4)
food color (p. 6)
candy corn

piping gels in tubes
small round candies (red-hot candies, Skittles®, etc.)

Roll dough to ¼-inch thickness. Each cookie requires one 2-inch circle for the body, one triangle for the tail, one ⅞-inch circle for the head, two small rectangles for legs, plus one long rectangle for the neck, if desired. (See p. 7 for cutter ideas.) Arrange shapes on a baking sheet. Press pieces together with lightly moistened fingers. Be sure dinosaurs are at least 2 inches apart. Follow baking and cooling instructions for large cookies (p. 7).

To decorate, spread Buttercream Frosting over tops of cookies. Press candy corn into frosting to form spines, holding spines in place until set. Use a variety of gels and candies to finish decorating. Refrigerate to set frostings.

ROBO-MONSTERS

(pictured on p. 16)

Basic Sugar Cookie Dough (p. 3)
Flow Frosting (p. 4)
food color (p. 6)
small candies (red-hot candies, candy-coated gum, candy corn, silver decorating balls)

red or black licorice laces, cut into short lengths
piping gels in tubes

Roll out dough to ¼-inch thickness. Each cookie requires one 2-inch x 1½-inch rectangle for the main body, plus several smaller rectangles for head, feet, and arms. (See p. 7 for cutter ideas.) Place main body parts on a baking sheet. Add smaller rectangles to finish forms, then press pieces together with lightly moistened fingers. Be sure monsters are at least 2 inches apart. Follow baking and cooling instructions for large cookies (p. 7).

To decorate, tint small portions of Flow Frosting to desired colors. Spread frosting evenly over cookies. Before frosting sets, add small candies and licorice laces for facial features, hair, and antennas. After frosting sets, use decorating gels to add a variety of colors, shapes, and designs. Refrigerate to set frostings.

BAKED INVADERS

(pictured on p. 17)

Basic Sugar Cookie Dough (p. 3)
white ready-to-spread frosting (p. 5)
green and orange food color (p. 6)

small candies (decorating sprinkles, silver decorating balls, Skittles®)
chocolate piping gel in a tube

Roll dough to 1/4-inch thickness. Each cookie requires one 2-inch circle and one oval 3 inches long. (See p. 7 for cutter ideas.) Place circle on baking sheet, then place oval across the center of the circle. Press pieces together with lightly moistened fingers. Be sure space ships are at least 2 inches apart. Bake and cool as directed.

To decorate, tint white frosting green and orange; spread green frosting smoothly over the top part of each cookie and orange frosting over bottom part. (See photograph.) Press sprinkles and other small candies into frosting to represent lights and windows. Outline cookies with chocolate piping gel. Refrigerate to set frostings.

CLOWN-AROUND PALS

(pictured on back cover)

Basic Sugar Cookie Dough (p. 3)
wooden craft sticks
white ready-to-spread frosting (p. 5)

decorating frostings in tubes
piping gels in tubes
variety of small candies

Roll dough to 1/4-inch thickness. Each cookie requires one 3-inch circle for the head, one 7/8-inch circle (cut in half) for ears, and various sizes of dough triangles and rectangles for hat shapes and tie shapes. (See p. 7 for cutter ideas.) Place large circle on baking sheet. Attach ears, hat, and tie. Press pieces together with lightly moistened fingers. Be sure clowns are at least 2 inches apart. Insert a wooden stick into each circle. Follow baking and cooling instructions for large cookies (p. 7).

To decorate, spread white ready-to-spread frosting over cookies. Press candy decorations into frosting. Use decorating frostings and gels to create facial features, hair, flowers, etc. Refrigerate to set frostings.

Who knows what wonderful creatures lurk inside every batch of cookie dough?

With the simple shapes shown in this book, dream up your own cookie critters.

Once they are baked and frosted, decorate your kooky confections with wild candy shapes and cosmic colors. These cookies are fun to make, yummy to eat, and great to give as presents! Use your imagination, have fun, and don't forget to share!

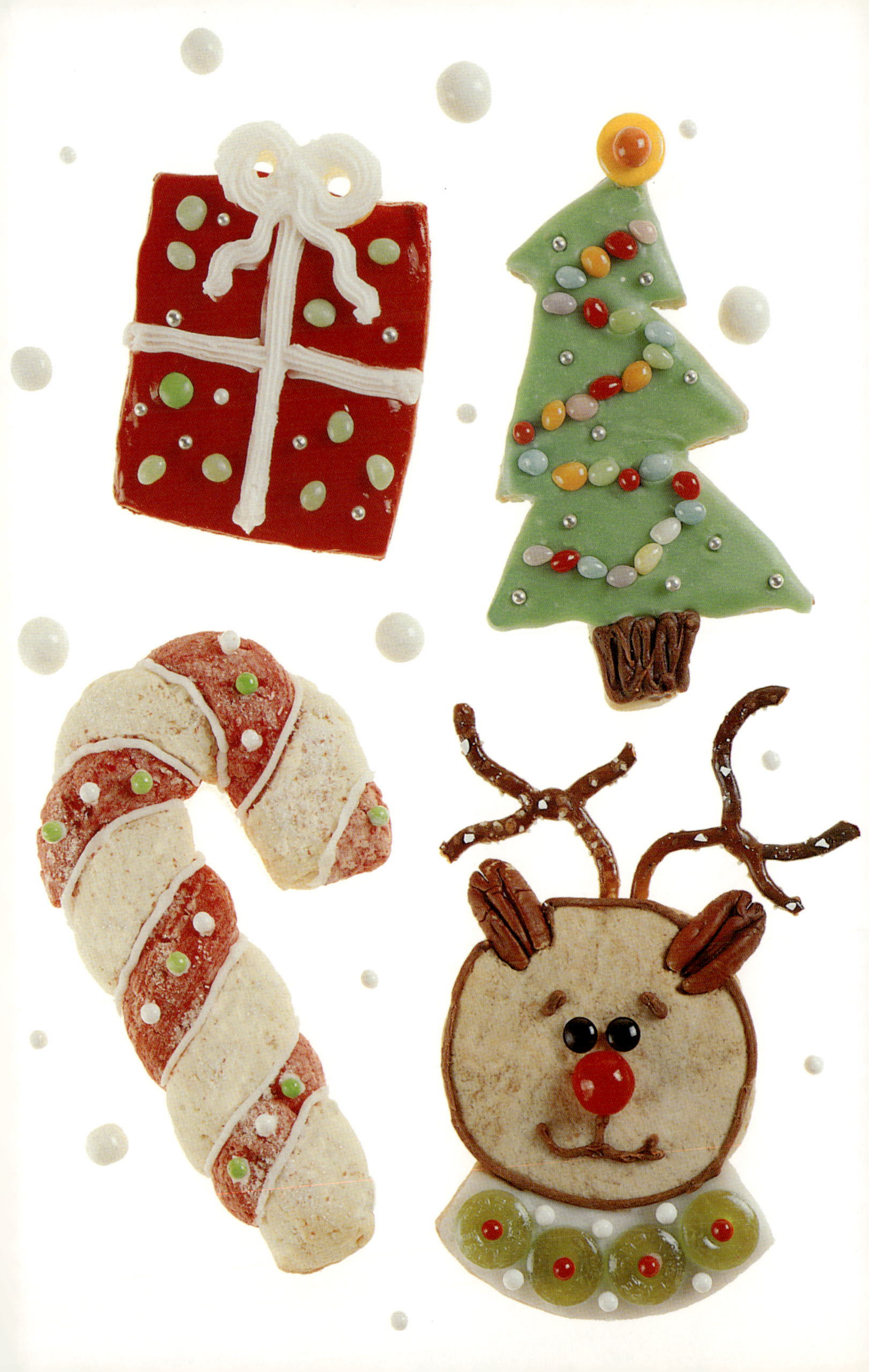

Holidays

Holidays are such busy times—and we strive to "do it all." This year, do it all, do it well, and do it easily. Every design in this section can be produced with purchased refrigerated cookie dough! Just slice and shape, then bake as directed on the package.

KRIS KRUMBLE

(pictured on front cover)

Basic Sugar Cookie Dough (p. 3)
Flow Frosting (p. 4)
red food color (p. 6)

small candies (gumballs, jelly beans, red-hot candies)
white decorating frosting in a tube

Roll dough to ¼-inch thickness. Each cookie requires two 2½-inch circles. (See p. 7 for cutter ideas.) Place one circle on baking sheet. Cut sides off second circle, leaving a rounded triangle (A). (See diagram.) Overlap triangle at top of the circle for hat (B). Curve the cut portions slightly to form crescents and place on circle to form mustache (C). Press pieces together with lightly moistened fingers. Be sure Santas are at least 2 inches apart. Follow baking and cooling instructions for large cookies (p. 7).

To decorate, tint half of frosting pink and half red. Spread pink Flow Frosting evenly on face area and red Flow Frosting on hat. Before frosting sets, add small candies for eyes, cheeks, nose, and pom-pon. After frosting sets, use white decorating frosting and star tip to decorate hat and sides of face. Using a leaf tip, pipe beard, mustache and eyebrows. Refrigerate to set frostings.

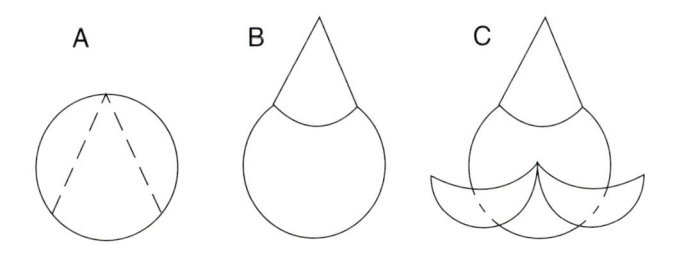

DANDY RANDY REINDEER

(pictured on p. 18)

Chocolate Sugar Cookie Dough (p. 3)
pretzel knots (2½" diameter)
pecan halves
Chocolate Buttercream Frosting (p. 4, optional)

small round candies (Life Savers®, gumballs, silver decorating balls)
chocolate decorating frosting in a tube

Roll dough to ¼-inch thickness. Each cookie requires one 2½-inch circle and one 2-inch rectangle. (See p. 7 for cutter ideas.) Place a circle on baking sheet. With floured fingers, shape rectangle of dough to form a collar. Press pieces together with lightly moistened fingers. Carefully break pretzel knots to resemble antlers. (See photograph.) Insert 2 pretzel pieces into top of each cookie for antlers. For ears, press 2 pecan halves to outside of pretzel pieces. Be sure deer are at least 2 inches apart. Bake and cool as directed.

To decorate, leave cookies unfrosted or spread Buttercream Frosting over tops of cookies. Attach small candies for eyes and nose with dabs of frosting. Spread chocolate decorating frosting on collar, then press candy "jewels" into frosting. Form mouth and eyebrows with chocolate decorating frosting. Refrigerate to set frostings.

PARTY PACKAGES

(pictured on p. 18)

Basic Sugar Cookie Dough (p. 3)
Flow Frosting (p. 4)
food colors (p. 6)

small candies (silver decorating balls, decorating sprinkles)
Buttercream Frosting (p. 4)

Roll dough to ¼-inch thickness. For each package, cut one 2½-inch square. (See p. 7 for cutter ideas.) Place packages at least 2 inches apart on baking sheets. Follow baking and cooling instructions for large cookies (p. 7).

To decorate, spoon equal portions of Flow Frosting into three separate containers. Tint each with food color to desired shade; cover tightly until ready to use. Working with one color at a time, spread Flow Frosting evenly over tops of several cookies. While frosting is beginning to set, spread second color of Flow Frosting on another set of cookies; follow the same procedure for third set of cookies. Working quickly, return to first set of cookies to add candies and sprinkles before frosting sets. Proceed in the same manner with the second and third sets of cookies. After frosting sets, use a star tip to pipe Buttercream Frosting across cookies to add the final touches of "ribbon and bows."

TASTY TREES

(pictured on p. 18)

Basic Sugar Cookie Dough (p. 3)
white ready-to-spread frosting (p. 5)
green food color (p. 6)
chocolate ready-to-spread frosting

small candies (red-hot candies, Skittles®, miniature M & M's®, silver decorating balls)

Draw and cut out from light cardboard, one triangle pattern 2 inches on each side, a second triangle pattern 1½ inches on each side, and a third triangle 1 inch on each side. Roll dough to ¼-inch thickness. Place cardboard patterns on top of dough. Using a floured table knife, cut around patterns. Each tree requires one triangle of each size, three triangles total. Cut one small square for the trunk of each tree. Arrangle triangles so they overlap slightly, then add trunk. (See photograph.) Press pieces together with lightly moistened fingers. Be sure trees are at least 2 inches apart on baking sheet. Follow baking and cooling instructions for large cookies (p. 7).

Tint white frosting with green food color. Spread green frosting over branch portions of cookies and chocolate frosting over trunk portions. Press a small yellow candy into the frosting at the top for a star and finish decorating by pressing small candies into frosting to create a garland.

COOKIE CANES

(pictured on p. 18)

Basic Sugar Cookie Dough (p. 3)
¼ to ½ **teaspoon peppermint extract (optional)**
red food color (p. 6)

decorating sprinkles or silver decorating balls
white decorating frosting in a tube

If desired, add peppermint extract when mixing dough. Divide dough in half; set one portion aside. Tint remaining dough with red food color. Cover and chill doughs until ready to use. For each candy cane, pinch off ½ tablespoon of dough from each portion. On a lightly floured surface, roll each to form a 6-inch rope. Place pieces side by side, then twist—lightly pressing ends together. (See diagram.) Place on an ungreased baking sheet, curving top to resemble a cane. Repeat with remaining dough, placing canes 1½-inches apart. Press candy "jewels" into dough. Bake until lightly browned, about 9 minutes.

To decorate, outline red stripes on cookies with white decorating frosting.

JIVIN' JACK O' LANTERN

(pictured on front cover)

Brown Sugar Cookie Dough (p. 3)
white ready-to-spread frosting (p. 5)
orange food color (p. 6)
green food color (optional)

candy corn
chocolate piping gel in a tube
green gumdrops (optional)

Roll dough to ¼-inch thickness. For each pumpkin, cut one 2½-inch circle. (See p. 7 for cutter ideas.) Place pumpkins at least 2 inches apart on baking sheets. Bake and cool as directed.

To decorate, color small amounts of white frosting with food color to make orange and green (optional) frostings. Set aside a small amount of orange frosting for piping; tint remainder of orange frosting a shade darker. Spread darker orange frosting over tops of cookies. Pipe ridges using light orange frosting. Press candy corn into frosting for eyes and nose. Using chocolate piping gel, outline pumpkin shape and pipe a jack o' lantern smile. Attach gumdrop with a dab of frosting or pipe a stem using green frosting. Refrigerate to set frostings.

SASSY SPIDER

(pictured on p. 24)

20 oz. (1 lb. 4 oz.) roll of refrigerated chocolate chip cookie dough*
chocolate ready-to-spread frosting
red or black licorice laces, cut in 2" lengths
miniature marshmallows
red-hot candies
green or yellow M & M's® (optional)
chocolate decorating sprinkles

Follow package directions for preparing and baking sliced cookies. Cool cookies thoroughly before decorating. For each spider, you will need 2 round cookies.

To make a spider, spread chocolate frosting over tops of two cookies. On one frosted cookie, arrange 8 pieces of licorice laces for legs, each extending about 1 inch beyond edge of cookie. Top with second cookie, frosted side up, to form a sandwich; press lightly. For eyes, press two marshmallows into the frosting and attach red-hot candy pupils with a dab of frosting. Or, press the edges of two M & M's® into the frosted cookie, standing candies upright. Gently press sprinkles into the tops of the frosted cookies. Allow frosting to set.

* Purchased 2-inch round, flat, soft cookies can be substituted.

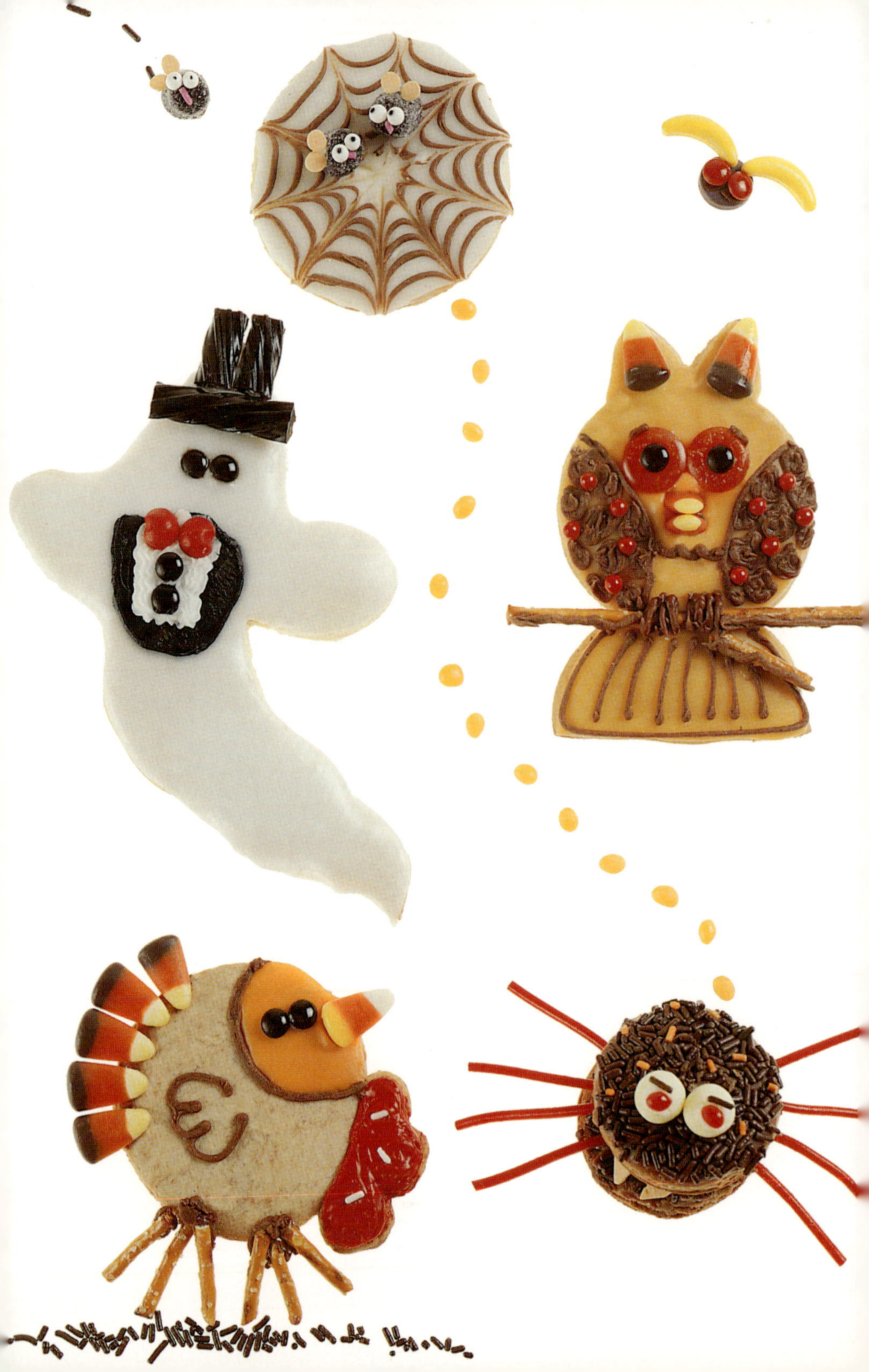

WACKY WEBS

(pictured on p. 24)

round, flat cookies of your choice, baked (p. 3) or purchased
Flow Frosting (p. 4)
chocolate piping gel in a tube

small black gumdrops (optional)
white decorating sprinkles (optional)

To decorate, spread Flow Frosting evenly over top of one or two cookies. (The frosting begins to set quickly, so decorate only one or two cookies at a time.) Immediately pipe circles of chocolate piping gel over frosting. Using a wooden pick, draw through the gel following directions of arrows shown in diagram. Decorate remaining cookies. Refrigerate to set frostings. Store in a single layer.

If you wish to add a "funny fly," press a gumdrop gently into the Flow Frosting before it sets. With a wooden pick, add a dab of frosting to the sides of the gumdrop and attach two decorating sprinkles for wings. Make eyes from two white sprinkles and attach with dabs of frosting. (See photograph.)

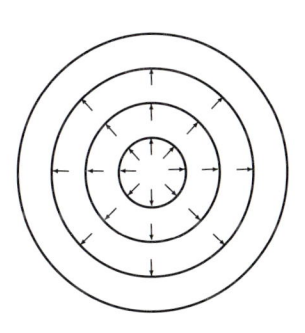

FORMAL PHANTOM

(pictured on p. 24)

Basic Sugar Cookie Dough (p. 3)
Flow Frosting (p. 4)
small round candies (red-hot candies, miniature chocolate chips)

licorice gumdrops, sliced
black licorice sticks
white decorating frosting in a tube

Roll out dough to ¼-inch thickness. For each phantom, cut one 4 x 3-inch rectangle. (See p. 7 for cookie cutter ideas.) Place rectangles 2 inches apart on baking sheets. With floured fingers form shape by pressing and pinching dough. (See photograph.) Follow baking and cooling instructions for large cookies (p. 7).

To decorate, spread Flow Frosting evenly over tops of cookies. Before frosting sets, add small round candies for eyes. Dip gumdrop slices into sugar, flatten with a rolling pin, then press into frosting for tuxedo front. For buttons, attach candies with dabs of frosting. Cut 1½-inch lengths of black licorice and attach with dabs of frosting for top hat. After frosting sets, pipe a ruffle around button edges with decorating frosting. Refrigerate to set frostings.

SPOTTED OWL

(pictured on p. 24)

Chocolate Sugar Cookie Dough (p. 3)
Flow Frosting (p. 4)
yellow food color (p. 6)
candy corn
orange Life Savers®

small round candies
pretzel sticks
ready-to-spread chocolate frosting (p. 5)
chocolate piping gel

Roll out dough to ¼-inch thickness. Each cookie requires one and a half 2½-inch circles for the body and tail and two small triangles for the ear tufts. (See p. 7 for cutter ideas.) Place the first circle on a baking sheet, overlap the half circle at the bottom, then attach triangles at the top of the circle. Press pieces together with lightly moistened fingers. Be sure owls are 2 inches apart. Bake and cool as directed.

To decorate, spread yellow Flow Frosting evenly over tops of cookies. Before frosting sets, attach candy corn ear tufts, candy eyes, and pretzel stick twigs. After frosting sets, spread chocolate frosting over right and left sides of cookie for wings. (See photograph.) Press small round candies into chocolate frosting for spots. Cut two candy corns in half with a knife, stand on end, points up, and attach with a dab of frosting for a beak. Using chocolate gel, pipe around the edge of the tail and detail the feet and tail feathers.

GOBBLE GOBBLERS

(pictured on p. 24)

Brown Sugar Cookie Dough (p. 3)
Flow Frosting (p. 4)
orange food color (p. 6)
small round candies
candy corn
chocolate piping gel in a tube
pecan halves (optional)
pretzel sticks
red decorating frosting in a tube
white decorating sprinkles

Roll dough to ¼-inch thickness. For each turkey, cut one 2½-inch circle and one free-form piece for a wattle. (See photograph.) Place a circle on the baking sheet and add wattle by overlapping pieces slightly. Press together with lightly moistened fingers. Be sure turkeys are at least 2 inches apart. Bake and cool as directed.

To decorate, leave partially unfrosted; spread orange Flow Frosting evenly over approximately ⅓ of the tops of cookies. (See photograph.) Before frosting sets, add two small round candies for eyes. Attach candy corn beak and "feathers" to the outside edge with dabs of frosting. After frosting sets, outline the face and wing with piping gel, or attach a pecan half with a dab of frosting for a wing. Attach three ¾-inch pretzel sticks with dabs of frosting for each foot. Using red decorating frosting, pipe a wattle on the free-form piece and add three white decorating sprinkles. Allow frostings to set.

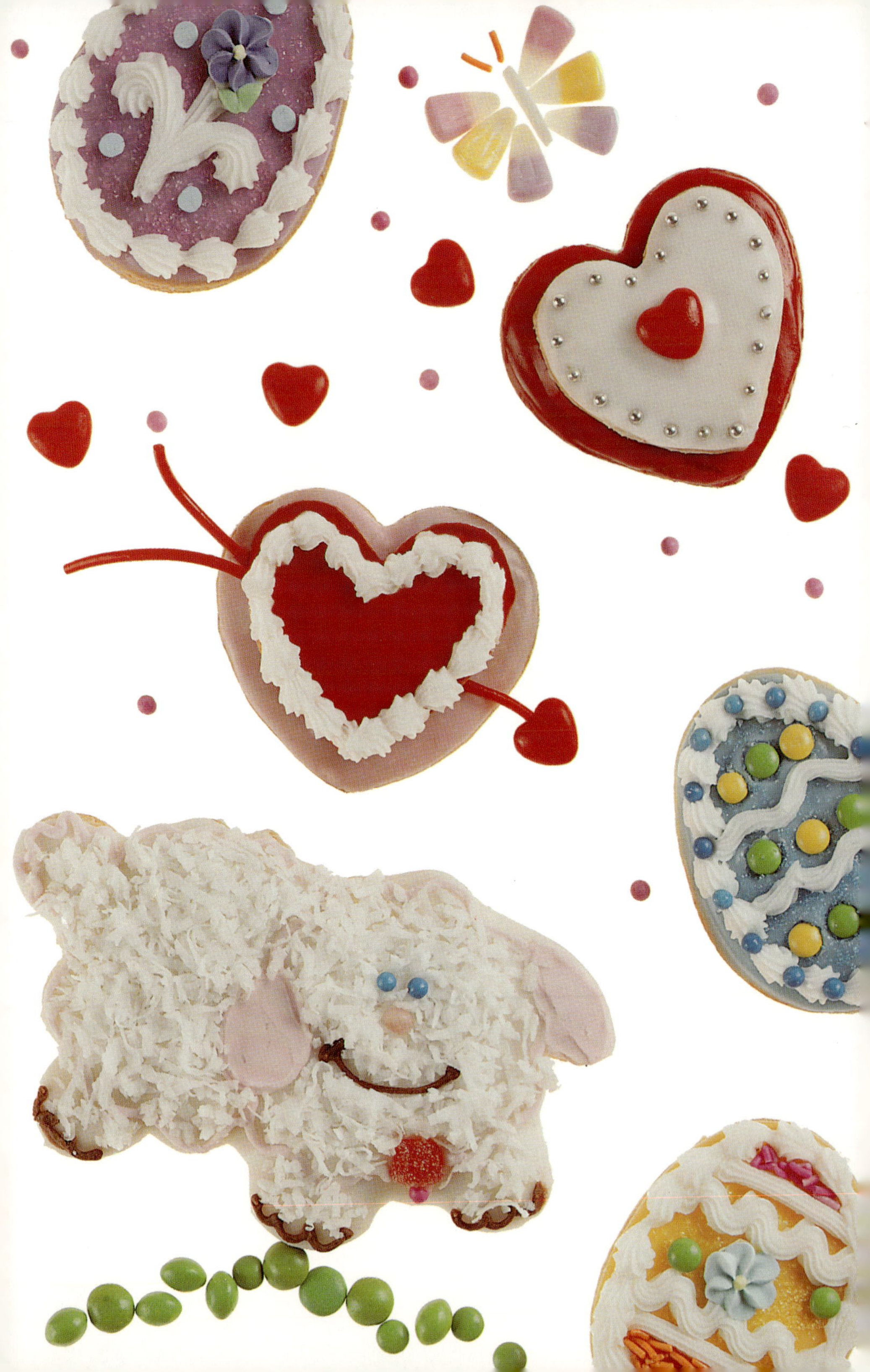

HAPPY HEARTS

(pictured on front cover)

Basic Sugar Cookie Dough (p. 3)
Flow Frosting (p. 4)
food color (p. 6)
small candies (tiny jelly beans, Runts®)

chocolate, pink, or white piping gel in a tube
white, red, or pink ready-to-spread frosting (p. 5, optional)

Cut out a heart pattern 2 inches in diameter from a folded piece of paper. Trace the shape onto light cardboard, then cut out. Roll dough to ¼-inch thickness. Place cardboard pattern on top of dough. Using a floured table knife, cut around pattern. Place hearts at least 2 inches apart on baking sheet. Bake and cool as directed.

To decorate, spread Flow Frosting evenly over tops of cookies. Before frosting sets, add various candy shapes and sizes to form funny faces. If desired, after frosting sets, use white or tinted frosting and a round tip to outline the heart, pipe a face, decorative design, or a message, such as "Be Mine" or "X" and "O" (hugs and kisses).

SWEET HEARTS

(pictured on p. 28)

Basic Sugar Cookie Dough (p. 7)
Flow Frosting (p. 4)
red, white, or pink ready-to-spread frosting (p. 5, optional)

small candies (silver decorating balls, decorating sprinkles, heart-shaped red-hot candies)
pink or white piping gel in a tube (optional)

Cut out a heart pattern 2 inches in diameter from a folded piece of paper. Cut a smaller heart pattern 1 inch in diameter from a second piece of folded paper. Trace shapes onto light cardboard, then cut out. Roll dough to ¼-inch thickness. Place cardboard patterns on top of dough. Using a floured table knife, cut around patterns. For each set of double hearts, cut one large heart and one small heart from dough. Place hearts separately at least 2 inches apart on baking sheets. Bake and cool as directed.

To decorate, spread Flow Frosting evenly over tops of cookies. Before frosting sets, place one small heart cookie on top of a larger heart. Add decorating balls, sprinkles, and candies. After frosting sets, decorate with contrasting colors of decorating frosting and use piping gel or a star tip to outline heart shapes.

CHEWY EWE

(pictured on p. 28)

Basic Sugar Cookie Dough (p. 3)
white ready-to-spread frosting (p. 5)
red food color (p. 6)

shredded coconut
small round candies (small jelly beans, Skittles®)
chocolate piping gel in a tube

Roll dough to ¼-inch thickness. Each cookie requires two 1½-inch circles, two small triangles for ears, and four small rectangles for legs and tail. (See p. 7 for cutter ideas.) Overlap two circles on baking sheet, then add legs, ears and tail. With floured fingers, round the pointed edges of tail and each ear. Press pieces together with lightly moistened fingers. Be sure lambs are at least 2 inches apart. Follow baking and cooling instructions for large cookies (p. 7).

To decorate, tint a small amount of white frosting to a pink shade and set aside. Spread white frosting over tops of cookies. Carefully frost lamb's ears with pink frosting. Press coconut into white frosting for wool. Press candy eyes and nose into frosting. Using chocolate piping gel, pipe a mouth, hooves, and center of nose. Refrigerate to set frostings.

NEST EGGS

(pictured on p. 28)

Basic Sugar Cookie Dough (p. 3)
Buttercream Frosting (p. 4)
food color (p. 6)

decorating frosting in a tube (optional)
small candies (decorating sprinkles, silver decorating balls)

Roll dough to ¼-inch thickness. For each egg, cut one 3-inch oval. (See p. 7 for cutter ideas.) Place eggs at least 2 inches apart on baking sheets. Follow baking and cooling instructions for large cookies (p. 7).

To decorate, leave some cookies unfrosted and spread colored Buttercream Frosting over tops of remaining cookies. Using a piping set or decorating frosting in a tube, pipe designs using a mixture of dots, lines, and stars on all the cookies. (See p. 6.) If desired, add a variety of small candies and decorating sprinkles.

BOW TIE BUNNY

(pictured on front cover)

Basic Sugar Cookie Dough (p. 3)
pink and chocolate piping gels in tubes
red or black licorice laces, cut in 2" lengths

small round candies (chocolate chips, white gumballs, jelly beans, red-hot candies)
Buttercream Frosting (p. 4, optional)
coconut (optional)

Roll dough to ¼-inch thickness. Each cookie requires two 2-inch circles and two small triangels for the bow tie. (See p. 7 for cutter ideas.) Place one circle on baking sheet and attach bow tie pieces. (See photograph.) Cut second circle in two and with floured fingers, shape each piece by pressing and pinching dough to form ears. Attach ears to head. Press pieces together with lightly moistened fingers. Be sure bunnies are at least 2 inches apart. Bake and cool as directed.

To decorate, leave unfrosted. Carefully spread pink gel down the center of each ear. Use chocolate piping gel to outline head, ears, and mouth. Add a dab of frosting to licorice laces and candies and press into position for whiskers, eyes, nose, and mouth. (See photograph.) If desired, begin decorating by carefully spreading white Buttercream frosting over tops of cookies, then press coconut into frosting for fur. Refrigerate to set frostings.